JOAN TOWER

WILD PURPLE
for solo viola

I always thought of the viola sound as being the color purple. Its deep, resonant and luscious timbre seems to embody all kinds of hues of purple. I never thought of the viola as being particularly wild. So I decided to try and see if I could create a piece that had wild energy in it and meet the challenge of creating a virtuosic piece for solo viola.

Joan Tower

Wild Purple was written for the violist Paul Neubauer who premiered the work at Merkin Concert Hall, New York City, September 1998.

duration ca. 7'

AMP 8153
First Printing: December 2001

ISBN 1-634-00731-9

Associated Music Publishers, Inc.

DISTRIBUTED BY

HAL•LEONARD®
CORPORATION
7777 W. BLUEMOUND RD. P.O. BOX 13819 MILWAUKEE, WI 53213

for Paul Neubauer
WILD PURPLE

Joan Tower

* Accel. al tremolo.

4

* Accel. al tremolo.

* Accel. al tremolo.

U.S. $12.99

HL50483608

Associated Music Publishers, Inc.

ISBN 978-0-634-00731-6